ONE MAN, TWO LIVES

BEYOND BORDERS

GAYATRI DADLANI

Made with ♥ on the Notion Press Platform
www.notionpress.com

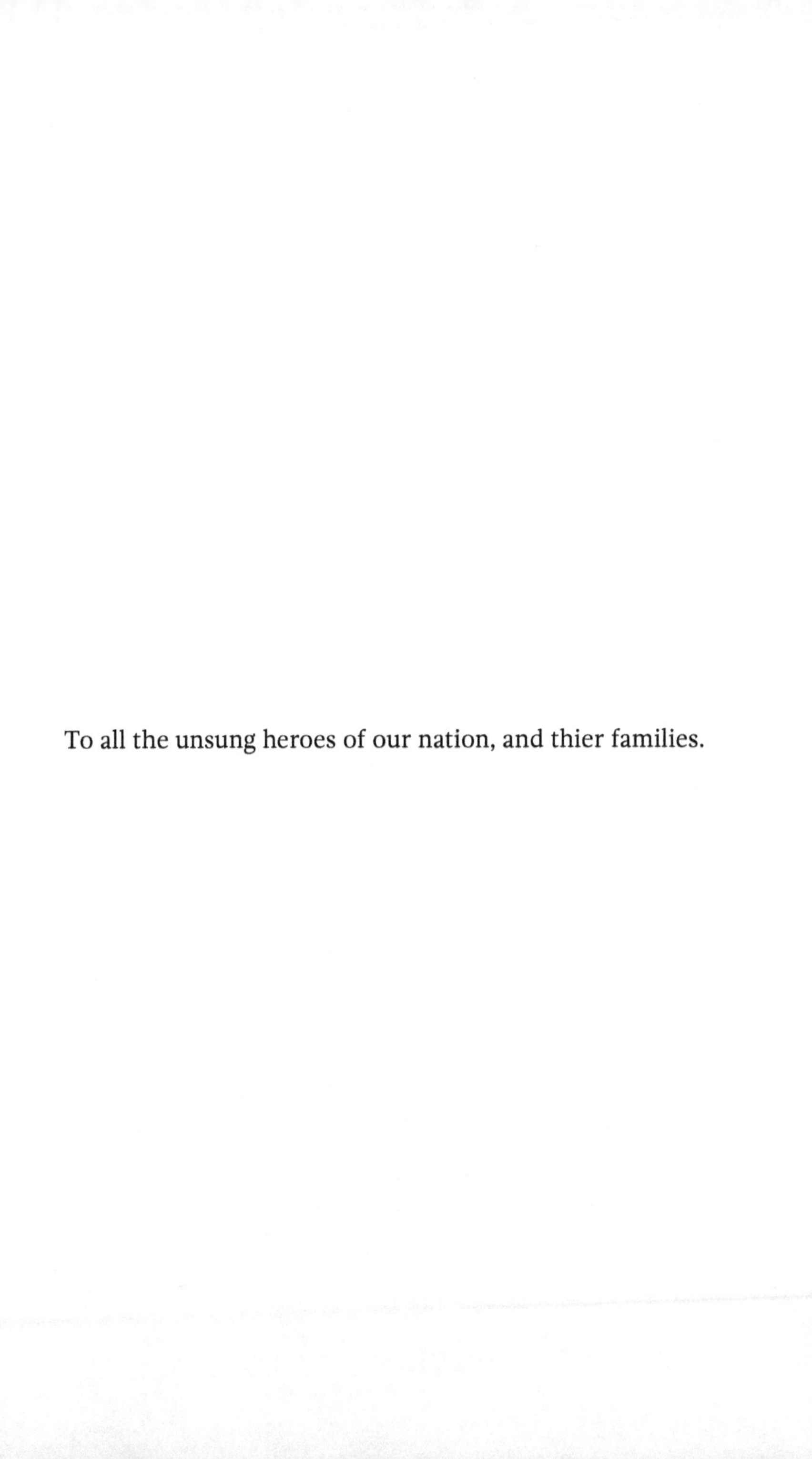

To all the unsung heroes of our nation, and thier families.

Contents

Preface

This story is about a amn who is a son, a true patriot, an actor, a spy and known as the "Black Tiger" to the Indian Intelligence. He was a legend, one of the greatest spy known to India. A Young boy who was onto a mission for his beloved nation, He was Ravindra Kaushik.

-Gayatri

Prologue

This is the story of Ravindra Kaushik, a young man, at the age of 23, who is onto live a life, which he had played on the stage of an theatre competition, a life full of torture is ahead him but still has his name edged in the espionage history of India. His life is more like a fiction story, known only to books, movies and dreams.

CHAPTER ONE

THE START

Ravindra Kaushik, born on 11th of April ,1952 into Sri Ganganagar, lying into the heart of Rajasthan's northern district, a district which has been through all dusty winds, sun's unrelenting power, gentle winter and heavy rains. Ravindra Kaushik, our *nation's "Black Tiger"* was just as same as standing strong in every situation. The story began when he was just 17 the man who was looked twice upon crossing and talked about, the reason to be popular among the knowns was never being wealthy.

He belonged from a family with a background full of values, his father J.M. Kaushik who was an Indian Air Force Officer embedded the certain values of patriotism, discipline and bravery telling him every now then that how he had a father who has always kept his nation the priority.

His mother Amladevi who had firmly believed that her son would surely change the world someday, the mother who had courage in her son and wore simplicity as her second skin.

Ravindra, who had belonged from a two-storied house which indeed did not speak of luxury, but every corner of the house reflected the people living in it. Studying as a student in a local government school, where he surely was the star pupil who had noticed the tiniest of bits, absorbed it all, even if it was the vendors on streets arguing about politics, the fascinating news mentioned in daily newspapers and radio or even more. Growing he had had a keen interest in theatre, when the sun used to hit the dusk, with orange lights covering the sky, Ravindra would transform into a character from Mahabharata on a day and the other into a freedom fighter against the British.

Ravindra was witness of the 1965 Indo-Pak war, living in a district on the border and having a father in the Indian Air Force, Ravindra knew much more than the ordinary, which had caused him to be more patriotic, and care for country. Who knew that this little child's mind diverted to patriotism would make someone great to the nation one day. His intent to help the soldiers on the border was denied due to his young age. Now, over the years Ravindra had become a great man with great values, with certain hobbies. He had studied at the Bihani P.G. College pursing the degree of Bachelor of Commerce, his great talent of acting had made a known person in the college, with his great acts, which would leave people startled with his acting skills, and the great storyline.

It was the time of the late 1970's. This day was not so ordinary like the others, with a stage act incoming for Ravindra. He had participated in the National Theatrical Festival hosted by the bustling city of Lucknow, Ravindra was prepared, deep into the role he was playing in his mono-act.

One of his favorite roles, the role which had his mind remember of the little him who had always wanted to be a soldier. The role of a spy for the nation, an espionage sneaked into China, who had given great information to its nation, staying there, one day, he was caught in China, surviving through the torture from the Chinese officers and then at last sacrificing his life to the nation.

After, the act was over there was silence, not one uttered a word, no claps, just an emotion that left people cry in tears openly was delivered by a mere 21-year-old college student following his hobby, performing on the stage. This authentic acting performance delivered by Ravindra was surely about to change his life, a plot upcoming in his life, a plot only known to the movies.

CHAPTER TWO

THE TURNING POINT

The performance surely had left the audience with a great memory of an talented young boy who would one day become an actor, be the reason for success of many movies in the Bollywood industry. But who knew fate and Ravindra clearly had some other plans. As the lights were dim, curtains closed, Ravindra back into the real one, after living the life and soul of a espionage. He was, unknown that his performance was witnessed by two RAW (Research and Analysis Wing) officials sitting in the crowd.

The RAW officials were in the lookout for of individuals with exceptional qualities which could help them. Through the performance the RAW officials realized how the acting skills, charisma, deep patriotism, delivered by Ravindra on the stage would fit right into the check boxes they had set for the man they were finding for. Here, the two lives were going fulfil their wishes one Ravindra, who had dreamt of being a figure who could help his nation through the tough times and the officials who were searching endlessly for the perfect person that could help them in their tasks. The deeply impressed RAW officials approached Ravindra without putting a second thought into the results. Though many questions would have risen, what if Ravindra had denied? What if the officials could change their mind? And many more the officials, just did not care about what was the second thought. Discreetly, the officials approached Ravindra, at the backstage, at first coaxing how great he performance how his sense of courage and patriotism which was shown just seemed to perfect to believe it was acting, after a bit knowing Ravindra's identity the officials were at relief, sure now that there is no one that could be more right for the role than this man. Without any further due told him how they had needed someone exactly like him, with the qualities that Ravindra had mastered.

Ravindra then being curious must've asked what exactly they had meant, in reply the officials must've told him about their real identity and how they were looking for a person who could cross the borders, provide them information and be a great use to them. It was truly something that Ravindra had ought to be. For the nation anything, now this man who was performing on a stage being an espionage, had his destiny take 360 degrees turn and was going to live it. 1973, that day marked a huge day in Ravindra's life.

This is where the actual story had begun with Ravindra being called to Delhi for the training, keeping it a secret from everyone, none should know about it, not even his parents. Lying seemed to be the best option for that situation, so he did. Lied to his parents that he was going to do a job in Delhi, to fulfil his duties as an employee. Takings blessings from his parents, love from siblings, he opted to carry his father's legacy forward of being a man loyal to the nation. **Now, Ravindra Kaushik, To be Nabi Ahmed Shakir.**

1975, the year Ravindra Kaushik successfully completed his training under RAW, completely became Nabi Ahmed Shakir. The past two years completed changed how he was defined, a devote Punjabi Hindu transformed to a Muslim with new identities and looks. The then, young Ravindra was now a diligent agent who was trained to face challenges, take risks, made more brave to withstand his fears, and hide his true identity. During these two years, Ravindra was made to do rigorous training to step up into Pakistan. His training had started with him learning Urdu, as he initially from Sriganganagar in Rajasthan belonging from a Punjabi roots, he was fluent in Punjabi which was understood by many Pakistanis. He was made to undergo training to be a devoted Muslim, learning their culture, traditions, aspects, and history. The things did not stop here he was trained under operational training, where he had learnt to use professional weapons, surveillance techniques, cryptography, and methods of clandestine communication. At last, he was made understood psychological espionage systems and mentally prepared for the interrogations and situations he may have to live in upcoming time.

All the hardships he had to go through would help him a lot in the future to provide information to the Indian officials staying in Pakistan, face situations and interrogations, be undercover, to build trust among the new environment as if he's one of them, ensure security and resilience in his work by commuting information securely by being a hostile in the other nation.

Although, he was never left on anything during his days of training, a major issue arrived which occurred even when he had a proper identification, that was, being unknown with any personal identification would be weird, so to act to this situation he was sent to Karachi University to pursue his studies in L.L.B his dedication during the studies there, made it better to solidify his identity. Now, that he had blend perfectly and seamlessly in Pakistan it was time to start for what he was there for initially. The real mission for his country, his nation, he was now onto it.

CHAPTER THREE

THE CAPTURE

Ravindra Kaushik operating under the Nabi Ahmed Shakir was now enlisted into the Pakistani army, started his operation, providing major information to the Indian playing his role very well. With the story continuing forward and plot waiting for the protagonist of this tale. Every ounce of hard work done by Ravindra was paying off. To solidify his strategic position, he was set of to marry a Pakistani woman named Amanat the daughter of man associated with the army-unit and they had a child together too.

Living a life full of difficulties but with success with his hard work at top. Nabi was now known as the major in the Pakistani army. Now, things were soon about change, with turns, and twists waiting for Ravindra further. Happy things do not last that long they say. This was felt true at that moment. When everything was going so right, suddenly Ravindra had lost contact with the RAW officials, no messages, no signal, neither any information or communication for a long time. When things were not in control anymore, the RAW officials had sent another undercover agent Inyat Masih to help build contact again with a special message to Ravindra. 1983, a crucial year in the plot of his life, where everything begins to not fall in place. Inyat who was sent to Ravindra for the better was caught by the Pakistan's ISI (Inter-Services Intelligence) she had to face many interrogations, torture and more. Under the pressure of the Pakistani officials she had revealed her identity, leading to uncover the identity of Ravindra too. Everything was ruined now, plans which were going smoothly, with great progress, were just past, strategies that were to be written in history.

Later, Ravindra was called for a pre-arranged meeting. Unaware of Inyat's capture, Ravindra started to head for the meeting just like he had always done. Upon Reaching, there, Ravindra was met with ISI officials. Then, Ravindra came to know that he was caught into a web, a web that he had made for the benefit, had him captured now. Ravindra knew that there's no going back from the situation. With the patriotism in his heart and the trust of RAW officials and the whole nation behind his back, he chose to face the situation.

CHAPTER FOUR

THE SILENCE

Ravindra Kaushik known as the *"Black Tiger"* to the Indian intelligence, the man who used to walk confidently in the corridors of Pakistani Armed Forces, now must face grim reality. He had found himself stuck in a deadly game of shadows.

After reaching the meeting room, Ravindra was taken to the interrogation centre in Sialkot, where he had endured brutal torture for two years, these two years, were surely the hard for Ravindra. Despite the stated facts, Ravindra chose to endure the physical and mental torment and did not bulge any information about India, knowing to protect the vital information and any identities and integrity of his mission. Ravindra clearly knew if he spilled any information about this mission or the information passed during these years, he could possibly put everyone in great trouble. Starting from 1983, a really hard time was suffered by Ravindra. Many trials, torture, and the ISI officials neglecting his personal well being and health. In result to all of this Ravindra had a deteriorating health and faced several health issues while being captured.

1985, Ravindra had to face a military trial, where he was sentenced to death. He must have thought it was all over now, his life, he had surely lived his dream, a stage performance becoming a reality, made his parents proud, and most importantly the brutal torture he had to face every day, everything was over. However, this sentence was later commuted to life imprisonment by the Pakistan Supreme Court.

During the next few years, Ravindra was transferred several times from Sialkot to Kot Lakhpat to Mianwali and back and forth.

18 years of imprisonment, that was what Ravindra had to go through, during these 18 years he had never really lost hi spirit of a true patriot, never spoke a word about his country, showed what true patriotism really is while being at the verge of dying, unsure when all of this would end. Living in closed cell with grey walls around, which would have stinked with the scent of iron bars just as if they were those forgotten dreams.

Ravindra, a great actor then, now, he was now no longer playing roles, rather lost himself to one. Then, Nabi Ahmed Shakir was now, just a man who is trapped between these four walls which was his world, no one beside him, nothing familiar to him. Who could tell he was the man which was one called the *"Black Tiger"* by the Indian intelligence. How could a numb and helpless bodied human be one? He had suffered for days, blend into weeks and then those weeks blending months to years. The darkness of cell he must have would not only have him tortured physically but mentally too, making him remember how things were when he was out in the colourful world rather than this darkness, when he out there performing on the stage, when he was living to dream, all the time when he was sharing a special bond with his parents, learning values, growing up, making mistakes and everything rather that living in a world which is so small that if he spreads out his arms it would end. The times when he would have closed his eyes it would take him back to Sriganganagar with the scent of roasted peanuts, ink of scripts written to the roles he would perform, the stage, his passion, the unexpected turns, highs and lows he had to go through during his life.

He was tired enough of his life, being so weak, helpless now after 18 years of torture. He wanted to communicate with his family, with no way left he wrote letters, unsure if they would even reach them one day, letters he wrote feeling loneliness all around, hoping to get an answer for the comfort he had needed, he had poured down his emotions, feeling worse than ever. Health issues, abandonment, anguish, he wrote about it all, in one of his letters he wrote *"Had I been American, I would have been out of this jail in three days"* expressing how bad he had felt being an Indian, belonging from a huge country, but nothing could have been done with such great deeds as a true patriot. *"Is this the reward for all the years I risked my life for my country?"* He wrote feeling bitterness, and the urge to meet his family again, to live his life again. His letters always served as a testament to his unwavering patriotism.

At the end there was nothing left for him but death, eventually it came, while captured in the Mianwali Jail, Pakistan, he had lost his life to illnesses of pulmonary tuberculosis and heart diseases. At the moment, in November 2001 the *"Black Tiger"* a name given by Indra Gandhi herself had sacrificed his life far away from his homeland for his homeland.

Epilogue

In the history of espionage, Ravindra Kaushik, a great name screams what sacrifice truly is, a symbol patriotism and dedication. A young boy, who knew nothing, still went to the enemy country far from his homeland, for his homeland, not knowing what really could happen in the future. His story remained largely buried until, Dalip Singh a reporter, bought it to light, with an article published in The Telegraph writing about his extraordinary contribution to the Research and Wing Analysis (RAW). Thanks to Dalip's dedication Ravindra's story reached a wider audience, ensuring that India's one of the greatest spies with this great deed does not remain forgotten and unsung. Till now, Ravindra's sacrifice has not been glorified on the big screen, his family continue to campaign his dedication and bring their family member's story to acknowledgment, his mother passed away in 2006, doing so and his brother R.N Kaushik remains to fight for the recognition. Being vocal, *"We don't want money. What we want from the government is recognition of the contribution by agents as they are the real foundation of the security system."* Had aid R.N Kaushik. Ravindra's nephew, Vikram Vashisth, has been actively involved in the case too trying that his uncle's story to be authentic and true. His poignant letters from prison reveal a man who, despite feeling abandoned, remained steadfast in his loyalty to India. Kaushik's story is a testament to the sacrifices made by unsung heroes who operate in the shadows, their valour often unrecognized. His legacy continues to inspire and serves as a poignant reminder of the profound costs of safeguarding a nation's security. His silence under interrogation was louder than a battlefield cry—it was the voice of a true patriot, one who placed his country's safety above his own existence. In a world quick to forget its silent sentinels, Ravindra Kaushik remains an immortal flame in the ever-watchful shadows of national security. The government has taken no action in proving Ravindra's sacrifice and bring it to acknowledgement.